Oceans of the World

The Atlantic Ocean

By Lauren Gordon

Table of Contents

A Starfish Book

SEAHORSE PUBLISHING

Teaching Tips for Caregivers:

As a caregiver, you can help your child succeed in school by giving them a strong foundation in language and literacy skills and a desire to learn to read.

This book helps children grow by letting them practice reading skills.

Reading for pleasure and interest will help your child to develop reading skills and will give your child the opportunity to practice these skills in meaningful ways.

- Encourage your child to read on her own at home
- Encourage your child to practice reading aloud
- Encourage activities that require reading
- Establish a reading time
- Talk with your child
- Give your child writing materials

Teaching Tips for Teachers:

Research shows that one of the best ways for students to learn a new topic is to read about it.

Before Reading

- Read the "Words to Know" and discuss the meaning of each word.
- Read the back cover to see what the book is about.

During Reading

- When a student gets to a word that is unknown, ask them to look at the rest of the sentence to find clues to help with the meaning of the unknown word.
- Ask the student to write down any pages of the book that were confusing to them.

After Reading

- Discuss the main idea of the book.
- Ask students to give one detail that they learned in the book by showing a text dependent answer from the book.

The Atlantic Ocean

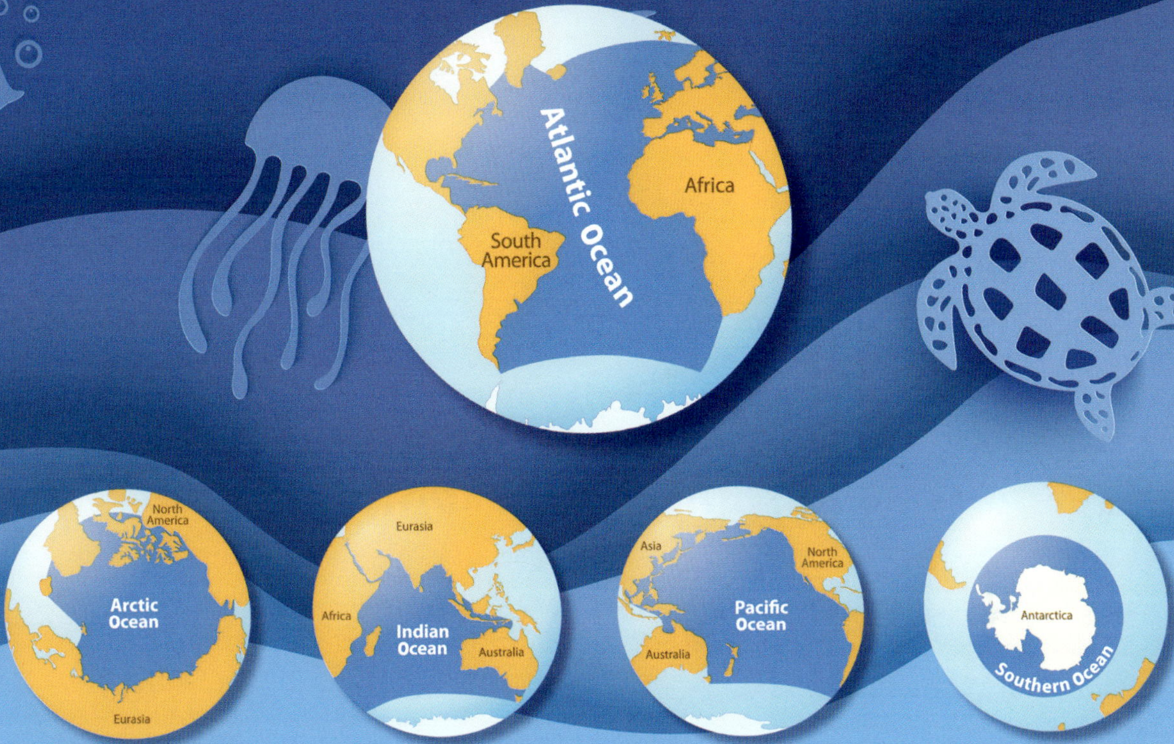

There are five oceans on Earth.
One is the Atlantic Ocean.

The Atlantic Ocean is huge!

It touches North America and South America on one side.

It touches Europe and Africa on the other side.

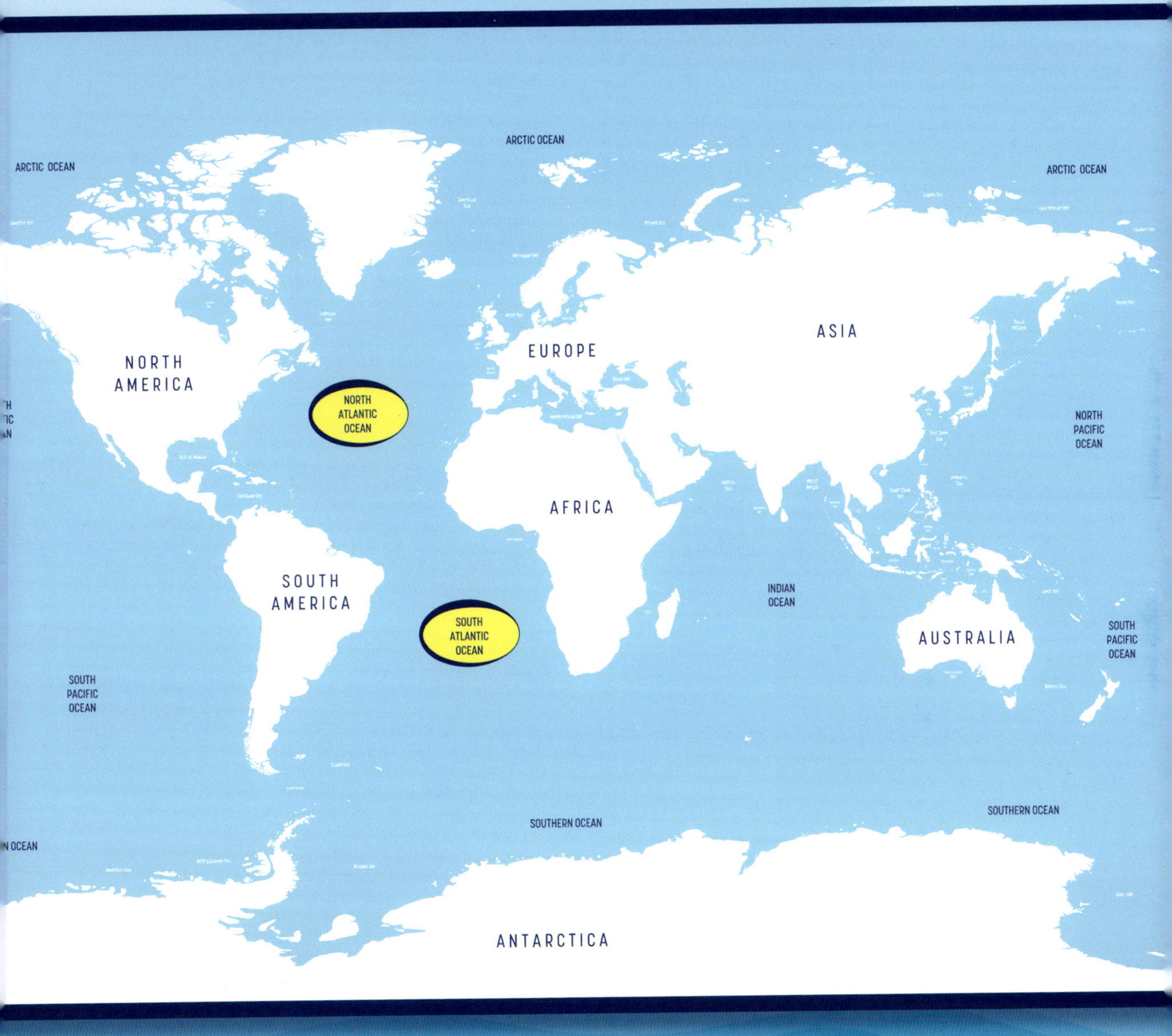
ARCTIC OCEAN
ARCTIC OCEAN
ARCTIC OCEAN
NORTH AMERICA
EUROPE
ASIA
NORTH ATLANTIC OCEAN
NORTH PACIFIC OCEAN
AFRICA
SOUTH AMERICA
INDIAN OCEAN
SOUTH ATLANTIC OCEAN
AUSTRALIA
SOUTH PACIFIC OCEAN
SOUTH PACIFIC OCEAN
SOUTHERN OCEAN
SOUTHERN OCEAN
ANTARCTICA

There are many **islands** in the Atlantic Ocean.

Some are cold and icy.

Some have palm trees.

The Bahamas and Iceland are countries found on islands in the Atlantic Ocean.

This is Atlas Titan. He is the reason we call it the Atlantic Ocean.

The word *Atlantic* comes from **ancient** Greek.

It means "sea of Atlas."

The Atlantic Ocean is the world's second biggest ocean.

It is about the same size as seven United States of Americas put together!

United States
Atlantic Ocean

The Atlantic Ocean
is very deep.

It can be up to 28,000 feet
(8,500 meters) deep.

That is over five miles
(eight kilometers) deep!

There are many types of animals that live in the Atlantic Ocean.

Some ocean animals have backbones, and some do not.

Animals with backbones are called **vertebrates**.

Manatees have backbones. Sea urchins do not.

The small North Atlantic octopus hunts at the bottom of the ocean.

It likes cold, deep water.

The North Atlantic octopus cannot survive in warm climates.

The Atlantic bluefin tuna is a fast ocean swimmer.

It is **endangered** because of overfishing in the Atlantic Ocean.

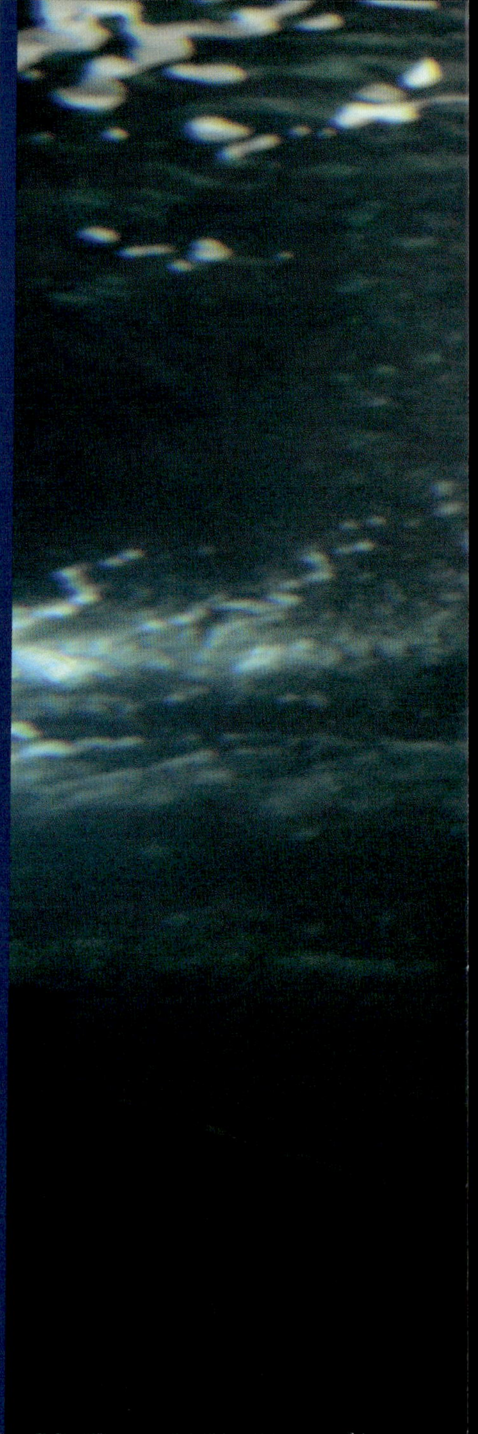

The population of Atlantic bluefin tuna is growing since laws have been made to protect it.

The Atlantic Ocean is in danger.

Pollution from humans is hurting the ocean.

It is important to reduce, reuse, and recycle to help our oceans stay clean.

Words to Know

ancient (AYN-shuhnt): very old

climates (KLYE-mits): usual or typical weather patterns in an area over a long period of time

endangered (en-DAYN-jurd): at risk of extinction, often because of human activity

islands (EYE-luhnds): pieces of land completely surrounded by water

pollution (puh-LOO-shuhn): harmful materials that damage air, water, and soil, including gases, chemicals, and smoke

vertebrates (VUR-tuh-brates): animals with a backbone

Index

Comprehension Questions

1. True or False: The Atlantic Ocean is one of three oceans in the world.
2. True or False: There are many islands in the Atlantic Ocean.
3. True or False: The Atlantic Ocean gets its name from Atlas Titan.
4. True or False: The Atlantic Ocean is two feet deep.
5. True or False: The Atlantic Ocean is in danger due to pollution.

Answers
1. False 2. True 3. True 4. False 5. True

About the Author

Lauren Gordon is originally from New York and now lives in Florida. She lives with her husband and two children. In her free time, she likes to read and spend time with her family.

Written by: Lauren Gordon
Design by: Jen Bowers
Editor: Kim Thompson

Photographs from Shutterstock.com: Cover and p.15 image ©2009 A Cotton Photo, backgound ©2012 Andrey_Kuzmin, water globe ©2012 zffoto; p.2 and throughout backgroud ©elic; p.3 and throughout background ©Aleksandra Bataeva, globes ©Designua; p.5 ©Pyty; p.6 ©2014 BlueOrange Studio; p.7 ©2019 Smit; p.8 ©2020 Rashbihari Dutta; p.11 ©2010 Chaykovsky Igor; p.13 ©2015 Rich Carey; p.15 ©2015 JGA; p.17 ©2015 Vladimir Wrangel; p.19 ©2019 jurgal photographer; p.21 ©2017 Richard Whitcombe

Library of Congress PCN Data
Oceans of the World / Gordon
The Atlantic Ocean
ISBN 978-1-63897-447-5 (hard cover)
ISBN 978-1-63897-562-5 (paperback)
ISBN 978-1-63897-677-6 (EPUB)
ISBN 978-1-63897-792-6 (eBook)
Library of Congress Control Number: 2021953381

Printed in the United States of America.

Seahorse Publishing Company
www.seahorsepub.com

Published in the United States
Seahorse Publishing
PO Box 771325
Coral Springs, FL 33077

SEAHORSE PUBLISHING